# First World War
## and Army of Occupation
# War Diary
## France, Belgium and Germany

48 DIVISION
Divisional Troops
Divisional Cyclist Company
3 December 1914 - 14 May 1916

WO95/2749/2

The Naval & Military Press Ltd
www.nmarchive.com
Published in association with The National Archives

Published by

## The Naval & Military Press Ltd

Unit 10 Ridgewood Industrial Park,

Uckfield, East Sussex,

TN22 5QE England

Tel: +44 (0) 1825 749494

www.naval-military-press.com

www.nmarchive.com

*This diary has been reprinted in facsimile from the original. Any imperfections are inevitably reproduced and the quality may fall short of modern type and cartographic standards.*

**© Crown Copyright**
**Images reproduced by permission of The National Archives, London, England, 2015.**

# Contents

| Document type | Place/Title | Date From | Date To |
|---|---|---|---|
| Heading | WO95/2749/2 48th Div Cyclist Coy April 1915-May 1916 | | |
| Heading | 48th Division 48th Divl Cyclist Coy Apr 1915-May 1916 | | |
| Heading | 48th Division 48th Divl Cyclist Coy Vol I From Dec 14 To 31 Aug 15 | | |
| Heading | War Diary Of South Midland Divisional Cyclist Company 48th (S. Mid) Divisional Cyclist Company From Formation of Unit Dec 3rd 1914 To August 31st 1915 Volume I | | |
| War Diary | | 03/12/1914 | 25/08/1915 |
| Heading | 48th Divl Cyclist Co Dec Vol III | | |
| War Diary | Bus Les Artois | 01/10/1915 | 31/10/1915 |
| Heading | 48th Cyclist Co Nov 1915 Vol IV | | |
| War Diary | Bus Les Artois | 01/11/1915 | 30/11/1915 |
| Heading | 1/1 Sth Mid Divn Cyclist Co Dec Vol V | | |
| War Diary | Bus Les Artois | 01/12/1915 | 31/12/1915 |
| Heading | 1/1st S.M. Divl Cyclist Co Jan VI | | |
| War Diary | Bus Les Artois | 01/01/1916 | 31/01/1916 |
| Heading | War Diary Of 48th Divl Cyclist Coy From Feb 1/1916 To Feb 29/16 Volume 7 | | |
| War Diary | Bus Les Artois | 01/02/1916 | 29/02/1916 |
| Heading | 48th Divl Cyclist Coy War Diary For March 1916 Volume 8 | | |
| War Diary | Bus Les Artois | 01/03/1916 | 26/03/1916 |
| War Diary | Couin | 27/03/1916 | 31/03/1916 |
| Heading | 48th Divisional Cyclist Coy War Diary For April 1916 Volume IX | | |
| War Diary | Couin | 01/04/1916 | 12/04/1916 |
| War Diary | St Ouen | 13/04/1916 | 13/04/1916 |
| War Diary | Acheux-En-Vimeu | 14/04/1916 | 20/04/1916 |
| War Diary | St Riquier | 21/04/1916 | 26/04/1916 |
| War Diary | St Ouen | 27/04/1916 | 27/04/1916 |
| War Diary | Couin | 28/04/1916 | 14/05/1916 |

WO95/2749/2

46TH DIV CYCLIST COY

APRIL 1915 - MARCH 1916

48TH DIVISION  BEF

48TH DIVL CYCLIST COY.
APR 1915-MAY 1916

121/6743

48th Division

48th Div: Cyclist Coy

Vol I

From Dec. 14 to 31 Aug. 15.

Original.

CONFIDENTIAL.

War Diary of

South Midland Divisional Cyclist Company.
afterwards known as
48th (S. Mid.) Divisional Cyclist Company.

From Formation of Unit Dec 3rd 1914

to August 31st 1915.

Volume I.

Confidential

War Diary of South Midland Divisional Cyclist Company.
Afterwards 48th (S. Mid.) Div. Cyclist Company.
Formed at CHELMSFORD on Dec. 3rd. 1914.

## 1914

**Dec. 3rd.** Following officers seconded for duty with this unit.

| | | |
|---|---|---|
| Captain | J. E. GROSVENOR | 7th Bn. Worcestershire Regt. |
| Lieut. | C. R. L. FALCY | 4th " R. Berkshire " |
| 2/Lieut. | F. F. G. BRENAN | 5th " Gloucestershire " |
| 2/Lieut. | L. E. KALKER | 7th " R. Warwickshire " |
| 2/Lieut. | G. D. B. BIRCH | 5th " " " |
| 2/Lieut. | R. S. PARTRIDGE | 6th " " " |
| 2/Lieut. | M. BOWEN | Bucks Bn. Ox. & Bucks. L.I. |
| 2/Lieut. | F. P. ROE | 6th. Bn. Gloucestershire Regt. |

Captain J. E. Grosvenor appointed Commanding Officer and attached 8th (Cyclist) Battalion Essex Regiment for 8 days instruction.

**Dec. 12th.** 15 to 20 other ranks detailed from each Battalion in the South Midland Division for

2.

duty with this unit, viz.

    5th Bn. R. Warwickshire Regt.
    6th  "   "      "           "
    7th  "   "      "           "
    8th  "   "      "           "
    4th  "   Gloucestershire   "
    5th  "      "               "
    6th  "      "               "
    7th  "   Worcestershire    "
    8th  "      "               "
    4th  "   Oxford & Bucks L.I.
    Bucks "   "       "     L.I.
    4th  "   R. Berkshire Regt.

From this date to January 17th 1915, training was conducted, though the men remained attached to their Battalions.

1915.

Jan. 18th. The Company assembled at GREAT TOTHAM, near WITHAM, ESSEX & went into billets; H.Q. were established at THE FABIANS.

From this date to March 30th, training

3.

took place with occasional work on road patrols in connection with East Coast Defences.

March 15th. 2/Lieut. L.E. KALKER broke his leg in a motor accident whilst on duty.

March 17th. Lieut. R.H. ABELL from the 8th Bn. Worcestershire Regt. joined the company in place of 2/Lieut. Kalker.

March 30th. The Company proceeded by train from CHELMSFORD to SOUTHAMPTON, and embarked for HAVRE.

March 31st. Arrived at HAVRE & proceeded to Rest Camp.

April 1st. Entrained at HAVRE.

April 2nd. Arrived at CASSEL & went into billets at S. MARIE CAPPEL.

J.L. Grosvenor
Captain

4.

April 5th. Proceeded by road to MERRIS & occupied billets.

April 7th. Lieut. C.R.L. Falcy, 2/Lieut. E.F.G. Brenan, 2/Lieut. M. Bowen & 60 N.C.O.s & men attached to IV Divisional Cyclist Company for 6 days instruction.

April 9th. Captain J.L. Grosvenor, 2/Lieut. R.S. Partridge & 2/Lieut. F.P. Roe with 60 other Ranks attached to VI Divisional Cyclist Company for 6 days instruction.

April 17th. Company moves station, by road to LA CRÈCHE.

April 18th. Company commences duty by providing traffic directing posts.

April 29th. All ranks who had not yet had trench instruction, proceeded to the trenches occupied by the Warwickshire Brigade.
Work commenced on redoubt on WULVERGHEM — MESSINES Road. Work on this redoubt was continued, first by night only, afterwards by day & by night until

5.

June 6th. One Sergeant & two privates sustained casualties, the former being serious.

May 2nd. Company moved billets to OOSTHOVE FARM near PLOEGSTEERT.

May 13th. Title of company changed to 48th (S. Mid.) Divisional Cyclist Company.

June 2nd. Lieut. C.R.L. Falay struck off strength of company on his attachment to R.F.C.
Lieut. R.H. Abell appointed 2nd in Command in lieu. of Lieut. Falay.

June 3rd. Company moved into camp near NIEPPE.

June 6th. Extract from Divisional Letter.
"The G.O.C. the Division considers that the best method of employing the Divisional Squadron & Divisional Cyclists during any operations that the Division may be called upon to undertake, is by the two working together. The two units

therefore, will in future be billeted together & for tactical purposes will be under the command of Major DICK, commanding "B" Squadron, King Edward's Horse. --- It is only by the closest co-operation of these two units that the important duties of the mounted troops can be carried out efficiently."

June 7th.    Div. Mtd. Troops inspected by Major General FANSHAWE, commanding 48th Division.
    Work on the Redoubt on WULVERGHEM — MESSINES road discontinued.
    Combined training with K.E.H. till June 25th.

June 18th.    2nd Lieutenant F. J. MARTIN, Army Cyclist Corps, joined for duty in lieu of Lieut. C. R. L. Faley.

June 27th.    The company moved station by road via VIEUX BEQUIN to BUSNES near LILLERS.

June 29th.    The company moved billets to BURBURE.
    Extract from London Gazette June 24th.
    5B. R. War. Reg. 2/Lieut G.D.B. Birch to be Temp. Lieut. To remain seconded.
    June 25th

## 7

July 1st.     Extract from Army Order 158. 1915.
The following Divisional Cyclist Companies of the Territorial Force will form part of the Army Cyclist Corps.
"The South Midland Divisional Cyclist Company."

From this date to July 17th, training was conducted with road reconnaissance of the IV Corps Area.

July 12th.     Extract from London Gazette
5th Bn. Gloucestershire Regt. 2/Lieut. E.F.G. Brenan to be temp. Lieutenant (March 29th)

July 19th.     The company marched to BERGUETTE Station & entrained for DOULLENS. Marched from DOULLENS to THIEVRES and bivouaced.

July 21st.     Training continued with road reconnaissance of VII Corps Area till August 4th.

July 22nd     Moved bivouacs to AUTHIE.

8

July 30th.   Observation Patrols sent out N. & S. of HEBUTERNE. Continued alternately with R.E.H. daily.
Moved bivouacs to BUS-EN-ARTOIS

July 31st.   "C" Platoon under 2/Lieut. F. P. Roe detailed to bivouac at, drain, improve, & form permanent guard over G.O.C.'s advanced dug out near HEBUTERNE.

Aug 5th.   ~~Bwed~~ Moved into billets at HEBUTERNE. Commenced work of draining and bricking BOYEAU DUGUESCLIN.

Aug 11th.   Extract from London Gazette. Aug 9th. "6th Bn Gloucestershire Regt. 2/Lieut. F. P. Roe to be Temp. Lieutenant & to remain seconded (June 16)."

Aug 24th.   Work on BOYEAU DUGUESCLIN completed.

Aug 25th.   Draining of BOYEAU JENA commenced.

121/7449

48th Kresowa

48th Div. Cyclist Co.

Dec

Vol III

Army Form C. 2118

# WAR DIARY
## ~~INTELLIGENCE SUMMARY~~
(Erase heading not required.)

Instructions regarding War Diaries and Intelligence Summaries are contained in F.S. Regs., Part II. and the Staff Manual respectively. Title pages will be prepared in manuscript.

| Place | Date | Hour | Summary of Events and Information | Remarks and references to Appendices |
|---|---|---|---|---|
| BUS-LES-ARTOIS | 1/10/15 | | Work on HEBUTERNE West defences continued. | |
| do | 2/10/15 | | do do do do | |
| do | 3/10/15 | | Observation posts continued. | |
| do | 4/10/15 | | Combined training with K.E.H. Manga Practice | |
| do | 5/10/15 | | do do do | |
| do | 6/10/15 | | Road repairing | |
| do | 7/10/15 | | do do | |
| do | 8/10/15 | | do do | |
| do | 9/10/15 | | do do | |
| do | 10/10/15 | | | |
| do | 11/10/15 | | Platoon training | |
| do | 12/10/15 | | do do | |
| do | 13/10/15 | | Road repairing | |
| do | 14/10/15 | | do do | |
| do | 15/10/15 | | do do | |
| do | 16/10/15 | | do do | |
| do | 17/10/15 | | (Transf from Lulu Cosyett. R. War. Regt. 2 Lt. R.S. Partridge to B Temp. 2 Lt. 9 Lt woman seconded. | |
| do | 18/10/15 | | Platoon training | |
| do | 19/10/15 | | do do | |
| do | 20/10/15 | | Roads repairing | |
| do | 21/10/15 | | do do | |
| do | 22/10/15 | | do do | |
| do | 23/10/15 | | do do | |
| do | 24/10/15 | | Platoon training | |
| do | 25/10/15 | | do do | |
| do | 26/10/15 | | | |
| do | 27/10/15 | | | |
| do | 28/10/15 | | Road repairing | |
| do | 29/10/15 | | | |
| do | 30/10/15 | | | |
| do | 31/10/15 | | Throughout the month Divisional Observation Posts were continually in connection with "B" Squadron K.E.H. | |

121/7636

48th Division

48th Cyclist Co.

Nov. 1915

Vol II

Army Form C. 2118.

# WAR DIARY
## or ~~INTELLIGENCE SUMMARY~~
November 1915

(Erase heading not required.)

Instructions regarding War Diaries and Intelligence Summaries are contained in F. S. Regs., Part II. and the Staff Manual respectively. Title pages will be prepared in manuscript.

| Place | Date | Hour | Summary of Events and Information | Remarks and references to Appendices |
|---|---|---|---|---|
| BUS-LES-ARTOIS | 1/11/15 | | Training | |
| | 2/11/15 | | do | |
| | 3/11/15 | | Road repairs and other Div. fatigues | |
| | 4/11/15 | | do | |
| | 5/11/15 | | do | |
| | 6/11/15 | | do | |
| | 7/11/15 | | Training | |
| | 8/11/15 | | do | |
| | 9/11/15 | | Road repairs and other Div. fatigues | |
| | 10/11/15 | | do | |
| | 11/11/15 | | do | |
| | 12/11/15 | | do | |
| | 13/11/15 | | Training | |
| | 14/11/15 | | do | |
| | 15/11/15 | | Road repairs and other Div. fatigues | |
| | 16/11/15 | | do | |
| | 17/11/15 | | do | |
| | 18/11/15 | | do | |
| | 19/11/15 | | do | |
| | 20/11/15 | | Training | |
| | 21/11/15 | | do | |
| | 22/11/15 | | Road repairs and other Div. fatigues | |
| | 23/11/15 | | do | |
| | 24/11/15 | | do | |
| | 25/11/15 | | do | |
| | 26/11/15 | | do | |
| | 27/11/15 | | do | |
| | 28/11/15 | | Training | |
| | 29/11/15 | | do | |
| | 30/11/15 | | | |

Throughout the month Div. Observation Job were continued in conjunction with "B" Squadron K.E.H.

J.E. Gorrien Capt
(a/) 48th (S.M.) Div Cyclist Co

1) Statistisches Ceplac Co.
Dec
vol XV

45,-

Army Form C. 2118.

# WAR DIARY
## or
## INTELLIGENCE SUMMARY
*(Erase heading not required.)*

Instructions regarding War Diaries and Intelligence Summaries are contained in F. S. Regs., Part II. and the Staff Manual respectively. Title pages will be prepared in manuscript.

1/1st SOUTH MIDLAND DIVISIONAL CYCLIST COMPANY

VOLUME
DECEMBER 1915

| Place | Date | Hour | Summary of Events and Information | Remarks and references to Appendices |
|---|---|---|---|---|
| BUS-LES-ARTOIS | 1/12/15 | | Road cleaning & other fatigues 9/15 | |
| | 2/12/15 | | " " " " 10/15 | |
| | 3/12/15 | | " " " " 11/15 | |
| | 4/12/15 | | " " " " 12/15 | |
| | 5/12/15 | | Road cleaning & other fatigues 9/15 | |
| | 6/12/15 | | " " " " 10/15 | |
| | 7/12/15 | | " " " " 11/15 | |
| | 8/12/15 | | " " " " 12/15 | |
| | 9/12/15 | | " " " " 9/15 | |
| | 10/12/15 | | " " " " 10/15 | |
| | 11/12/15 | | " " " " 11/15 | |
| | 12/12/15 | | Road cleaning & other fatigues 9/15 | |
| | 13/12/15 | | " " " " 10/15 | |
| | 14/12/15 | | " " " " 11/15 | |
| | 15/12/15 | | " " " " 12/15 | |
| | 16/12/15 | | " " " " 9/15 | |
| | 17/12/15 | | Road cleaning & other fatigues 9/15 | |
| | 18/12/15 | | " " " " 10/15 | |
| | 19/12/15 | | " " " " 11/15 | |
| | 20/12/15 | | " " " " 12/15 | |
| | 21/12/15 | | " " " " 9/15 | |
| | 22/12/15 | | " " " " 10/15 | |
| | 23/12/15 | | " " " " 11/15 | |
| | 24/12/15 | | " " " " 12/15 | |
| | 25/12/15 | | Road cleaning & other fatigues 9/15 | |
| | 26/12/15 | | " " " " 10/15 | |
| | 27/12/15 | | " " " " 11/15 | |
| | 28/12/15 | | " " " " 12/15 | |
| | 29/12/15 | | " " To the Platoon attached 4th Battalion R. WARWICKSHIRE REGT for instruction in trenches E. of FONQUEVILLERS 9/15 | |
| | 30/12/15 | | " " | |
| | 31/12/15 | | " " | |

Throughout the month Div¹ Observation Posts were continued in conjunction with "B" Squadron K.E.H.

A.J. Grosvenor

1/15 S.M. Dime Cycliers Co.

Jan / VI

$8 in

Army Form C. 2118.

# WAR DIARY
## for
## INTELLIGENCE SUMMARY
(Erase heading not required.)

| Place | Date | Hour | Summary of Events and Information | Remarks and references to Appendices |
|---|---|---|---|---|
| BUS-LES-ARTOIS | JAN. 1 | | One platoon went into Trenches S.E. of FONCQUEVILLERS with 1/4 & 8th Batt. R. WARWICKSHIRE REGT. Road work with working pts 2 fatigues | |
| " | " 2 | | " | |
| " | " 3 | | " | |
| " | " 4 | | " | |
| " | " 5 | | " | |
| " | " 6 | | " | |
| " | " 7 | | " | |
| " | " 8 | | " | |
| " | " 9 | | " | |
| " | " 10 | | " | |
| " | " 11 | | " | |
| " | " 12 | | " | |
| " | " 13 | | " | |
| " | " 14 | | " | |
| " | " 15 | | " | |
| " | " 16 | | " | |
| " | " 17 | | " | |
| " | " 18 | | " | |
| " | " 19 | | " | |
| " | " 20 | | " | |
| " | " 21 | | " | |
| " | " 22 | | " | |
| " | " 23 | | " | |
| " | " 24 | | The Company received an Alarm at about 3.40am They stood to till 4.30am were then dismissed | |
| " | " 25 | | " | |

Army Form C. 2118.

# WAR DIARY
## for JANUARY
## INTELLIGENCE SUMMARY

*(Erase heading not required.)*

Instructions regarding War Diaries and Intelligence Summaries are contained in F.S. Regs., Part II. and the Staff Manual respectively. Title pages will be prepared in manuscript.

| Place | Date | Hour | Summary of Events and Information | Remarks and references to Appendices |
|---|---|---|---|---|
| BUS-LES-ARTOIS | JAN 26 | | One platoon went into trenches S.E. of FONCQUEVILLERS with 7th & 8th Batts. R.WARWICKSHIRE REGT. Road work rather Bn's fatigues. | |
| " | " 27 | | " " " " " " " " " " " " " " " " " " | |
| | | | The Company received a Gas Alarm at about 8 p.m. One platoon was sent at 8.45 p.m. to man SOUTH DOWN FORT. East of COLINCAMPS. An Officers patrol of 12 men was sent to HEBUTERNE to maintain communication in conjunction with a cavalry patrol. | |
| " | " 28 | | One platoon went into trenches S.E. of FONCQUEVILLERS with 7th & 8th Batts. R.WARWICKSHIRE REGT. Road work rather Bn's fatigues. | |
| " | " 29 | | " " " " " " " " " " " " " " " " " " | |
| " | " 30 | | " " " " " " " " " " " " " " " " " " | |
| " | " 31 | | The Company having been relieved 3rd several Bn's fatigues, 3 platoons commenced a 10 days Course of training. | |
| | | | Throughout the month Div. Observation Posts were continued in conjunction with "B" Squadron, King Edward Horse. | |

1353  Wt. W3544/1454  700,000  5/15  D. D. & L.   A.D.S.S./Forms/C. 2118.

CONFIDENTIAL

War Diary
of
48th Divl. Cyclist Coy

From Feb 1/1916 to Feb 29/16

Volume 7.

Appendix to Vol VI

Army Form C. 2118.

# WAR DIARY
## for February
## INTELLIGENCE SUMMARY.
(Erase heading not required.)

Instructions regarding War Diaries and Intelligence Summaries are contained in F. S. Regs., Part II. and the Staff Manual respectively. Title pages will be prepared in manuscript.

| Place | Date | Hour | Summary of Events and Information | Remarks and references to Appendices |
|---|---|---|---|---|
| BUS-LES-ARTOIS | 1/2/16 | | 10 days course of training continued (2nd day) | |
| | 2/2/16 | | Course of training discontinued. Company employed on Div'l fatigues | |
| | 3/2/16 | | Company employed on Div'l fatigues | |
| | 4/2/16 | | do | |
| | 5/2/16 | | do | |
| | 6/2/16 | | do | |
| | 7/2/16 | | do | |
| | 8/2/16 | | do | |
| | 9/2/16 | | do | |
| | 10/2/16 | | do | |
| | 11/2/16 | | do | |
| | 12/2/16 | | do | |
| | 13/2/16 | | do | |
| | 14/2/16 | | Two Platoons held in constant readiness to turn out as Mobile Div'l Reserve. The others carry on training within the Billeting area. Remainder of Company on Div'l fatigues. | |
| | 15/2/16 | | do | |
| | 16/2/16 | | do | |
| | 17/2/16 | | do | |
| | 18/2/16 | | do | |
| | 19/2/16 | | do | |
| | 19/2/16 | 6.20pm | Company ordered to stand by. Officers tabed on duty. See diary 1st days of cross/road N.15.C. S.1. Capt. with instructions to report any activity in the neighbourhood of FONQUEVILLERS | Sheet 57D |

#353 Wt. W3544/1454 700,000 5/15 D. D. & L. A.D.S.S./Forms/C. 2118.

Army Form C. 2118.

# WAR DIARY
## for
## INTELLIGENCE SUMMARY.

*(Erase heading not required.)*

Instructions regarding War Diaries and Intelligence Summaries are contained in F. S. Regs., Part II. and the Staff Manual respectively. Title pages will be prepared in manuscript.

*[Stamp: 1/1st SOUTH MIDLAND DIVISIONAL CYCLIST COMPANY — No. VOLUME 1 — Date 2/3/16]*

| Place | Date | Hour | Summary of Events and Information | Remarks and references to Appendices |
|---|---|---|---|---|
| BUS-LES-ARTOIS | 20/2/16 | | Two platoons kept in constant readiness to turn out as mobile Div. Reserve. These platoons carry on training within the Billeting Area. Remainder of Company on Div. fatigues. | |
| | 21/2/16 | | do      do      do      do      do | do |
| | 22/2/16 | | do      do      do      do      do | do |
| | 23/2/16 | | do      do      do      do      do | do |
| | 24/2/16 | | do      do      do      do      do | do |
| | 25/2/16 | | do      do      do      do      do | do |
| | 26/2/16 | | do      do      do      do      do | do |
| | 27/2/16 | | do      do      do      do      do | do |
| | 28/2/16 | | do      do      do      do      do | do |
| | 29/2/16 | | do      do      do      do      do | do |

Throughout the month Div. Observation Post were continued in conjunction with "B" Squadron, King Edwards Horse.

*[signature]*
Lieut & Capt.
Commanding

Original

48th Divl Cyclist Coy

War Diary for
MARCH 1916.
Volume

Army Form C. 2118.

Original

# WAR DIARY
## or *March*
## INTELLIGENCE SUMMARY.
*(Erase heading not required.)*

Instructions regarding War Diaries and Intelligence Summaries are contained in F. S. Regs., Part II. and the Staff Manual respectively. Title pages will be prepared in manuscript.

| Place | Date | Hour | Summary of Events and Information | Remarks and references to Appendices |
|---|---|---|---|---|
| BUS-LÉS-ARTOIS | 1/3/16 | | Two platoons kept in reserve to turn out as mobile first Reserve these platoons sleep in training building the billeting area. Remainder of Company on first Fatigue. | |
| | 2/3/16 | | do | do |
| | 3/3/16 | | do | do |
| | 4/3/16 | | do | do |
| | 5/3/16 | | do | do |
| | 6/3/16 | | do | do |
| | 7/3/16 | | do | do |
| | 8/3/16 | | do | do |
| | 9/3/16 | | do | do |
| | 10/3/16 | | do | do |
| | 11/3/16 | | do | do |
| | 12/3/16 | | do | do |
| | 13/3/16 | | do | do |
| | 14/3/16 | | do | do |
| | 15/3/16 | | do | do |
| | 16/3/16 | | do | do |
| | 17/3/16 | | do | do |
| | 18/3/16 | | do | do |
| | 19/3/16 | | do | do |
| | 20/3/16 | | do | do |
| | 21/3/16 | | do | do |
| | 22/3/16 | | do | do |

# WAR DIARY
## INTELLIGENCE SUMMARY

Army Form C. 2118.

| Place | Date | Hour | Summary of Events and Information | Remarks and references to Appendices |
|---|---|---|---|---|
| BUS-LES-ARTOIS | 23/3/16 | | Two platoons kept on carrying materials to dugouts & two platoons were employed in making the bullet-proof loopholes & carrying them up to the front line | |
| | 24/3/16 | | do | |
| | 25/3/16 | | do | |
| | 26/3/16 | | Company moved to billets in huts at COIGNEUX | |
| COIGNEUX | 27/3/16 | | Two platoons of the company were employed in carrying down the billets from Kismere & two platoons of fatigue | |
| | 28/3/16 | | do | |
| | 29/3/16 | | do | |
| | 30/3/16 | | do | |
| | 31/3/16 | | Last of Riemen hutments were taken to 16th Division | |
|  |  |  | During the month Dust Showers Pits were constructed in conjunction with "B" Squadron all ranks have contributed |  |

Lt B.W. Offer
Lt 1st Sussex Cyclists

Original

CONFIDENTIAL

48th Divisional Cyclist Coy

War Diary

for

April 1916

Volume XVIII IX

Original

CONFIDENTIAL

Army Form C. 2118.

# WAR DIARY
## or
## INTELLIGENCE SUMMARY.

*(Erase heading not required.)*

Instructions regarding War Diaries and Intelligence Summaries are contained in F. S. Regs., Part II. and the Staff Manual respectively. Title pages will be prepared in manuscript.

| Place | Date | Hour | Summary of Events and Information | Remarks and references to Appendices |
|---|---|---|---|---|
| COUIN | 1/4/16 | | Two platoons kept in readiness to turn out as Mobile Divl. Reserve. These platoons carry on training within the billeting area. Remainder of Company on divl. fatigues. | |
| | 2/4/16 | | One platoon kept as mobile Divl. Reserve. This platoon trains within the billeting area, not as Mobile Divl. Reserve. The platoon attached to 5th Batt. gloster regt. in the trenches on HEBUTERNE-SERRE ROAD for 48 hours. Remainder of Company on Divl. fatigue. | |
| | 3/4/16 | | do | |
| | 4/4/16 | | do | |
| | 5/4/16 | | One platoon kept in readiness to turn out as mobile Divl. Reserve. This platoon carries on training within the billeting area. One platoon attached to 13th Batt. Royal Berkshire Regt. in the trenches on HEBUTERNE-SERRE ROAD for 48 hours. Remainder of Company on Divl. fatigues. | |
| | 6/4/16 | | do | |
| | 7/4/16 | | do | |
| | 8/4/16 | | do | |
| | 9/4/16 | | do | |
| | 10/4/16 | | do | |
| | 11/4/16 | | One platoon kept in readiness to turn out as Mobile Divl. Reserve. Remainder of Company training within the billeting area. "B" Squadron R.E.M. Company was taken off divl. fatigues to prepare for move on following day. Divl. Mounted troops Observation post was withdrawn from HEBUTERNE. | |
| ST OUEN | 12/4/16 | | Company marched with "B" Squadron KING EDWARDS HORSE as Divl. Mounted troops to ST OUEN | |
| | 13/4/16 | | Company marched with do to ACHEUX EN YIMEU | |

and attd to SECUNDERABAD BRIGADE, 2nd INDIAN CAVALRY DIVISION for training

[signature]

Original
Confidential

Army Form C. 2118.

# WAR DIARY
## for April
## INTELLIGENCE SUMMARY.

(Erase heading not required.)

Instructions regarding War Diaries and Intelligence Summaries are contained in F. S. Regs., Part II. and the Staff Manual respectively. Title pages will be prepared in manuscript.

1/1st SOUTH MIDLAND DIVISIONAL
CYCLIST COMPANY

| Place | Date | Hour | Summary of Events and Information | Remarks and references to Appendices |
|---|---|---|---|---|
| ACHEUX (ENVIRONS) | 14/4/16 | | Training with SECUNDERABAD BRIGADE. | |
| | 15/4/16 | | do | |
| | 16/4/16 | | do | |
| | 17/4/16 | | do | |
| | 18/4/16 | | do | |
| | 19/4/16 | | do | |
| | 20/4/16 | | Marched with do to ST RIQUIER. | |
| ST RIQUIER | 21/4/16 | | Training with do | |
| | 22/4/16 | | do | |
| | 23/4/16 | | do | |
| | 24/4/16 | | do | |
| | 25/4/16 | | do | |
| | 26/4/16 | | Left SECUNDERABAD CAVALRY BRIGADE and marched to ST OWEN | |
| ST OWEN | 27/4/16 | | Marched to COUIN and rejoined 48th DIVISION receiving some instruments as we were left on 13th April last for cleaning equipment etc. | |
| COUIN | 28/4/16 | | | |
| | 29/4/16 | | One Platoon left in readiness to turn out as Mobile Strike Force. This Platoon carries on training within the billeting area. Remainder of Company training and Range Practice | |
| | 30/4/16 | | do do | |

# WAR DIARY
## for MAY
## INTELLIGENCE SUMMARY

*(Erase heading not required.)*

Army Form C. 2118.

Instructions regarding War Diaries and Intelligence Summaries are contained in F.S. Regs., Part II. and the Staff Manual respectively. Title pages will be prepared in manuscript.

| Place | Date | Hour | Summary of Events and Information | Remarks and references to Appendices |
|---|---|---|---|---|
| COUIN | 1/5/16 | | Bn. Fatigues, Range practice and Training. One platoon kept in readiness to turn out as Bn. Mobile Reserve | |
| " | 2/5/16 | | " " " " | |
| " | 3/5/16 | | " " " " One platoon inoculated against Typhoid. | |
| " | 4/5/16 | | " " and Training. One platoon kept in readiness to turn out as Bn. Mobile Reserve | |
| " | 5/5/16 | | " " " " | |
| " | 6/5/16 | | One platoon inoculated against Typhoid | |
| " | 7/5/16 | | Bn. Fatigues. One platoon kept in readiness to turn out as Bn. Mobile Reserve. | |
| " | 8/5/16 | | " " " " | |
| " | 9/5/16 | | " " " " | |
| " | 10/5/16 | | " " " " | |
| " | 11/5/16 | | " " " " | |
| " | 12/5/16 | | " " " " | |
| " | 13/5/16 | | Cleaning up for move | |
| " | 14/5/16 | | Moved to BEAUVAL S.N.E. & became part of VIII Corps Gdst Battalion | |

End of War Diary

www.ingramcontent.com/pod-product-compliance
Lightning Source LLC
Chambersburg PA
CBHW081249170426
43191CB00037B/2098